AIRPLANES

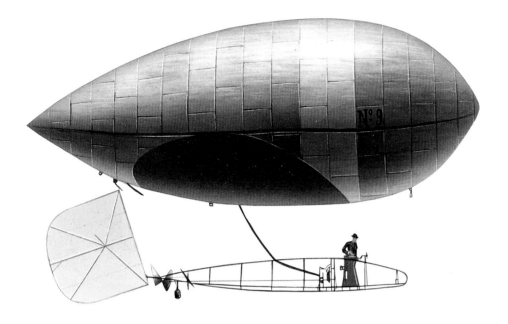

A Firefly Book

Published by Firefly Books Ltd. 2006

First printing

Published in the United States by
Firefly Books (U.S.) Inc.
P.O. Box 1338, Ellicott Station
Buffalo, New York 14205

Published in Canada by
Firefly Books Ltd.
66 Leek Crescent
Richmond Hill, Ontario L4B 1H1

Created and produced in Italy by
McRae Books
Borgo Santa Croce
8 – 50122, Florence

Series Editor: Anne McRae
Illustrations: Leonello Calvetti, Lorenzo Cecchi and Studio Stalio (Alessandro Cantucci, Fabiano Fabbrucci, Andrea Morandi)
Graphic Design: Marco Nardi
Editing and Picture Research: Chris Hawkes
Repro: Litocolor, Florence
Photos p. 12 © NASA

ISBN 13: 978-1-55407-134-0

Printed in Italy

Publisher Cataloging-in-Publication Data (U.S.)

Oxlade, Chris.
   Airplanes : uncovering technology / Chris Oxlade.
[52] p. : col. ill. ; cm.
Includes index.
Summary: Illustrated guide to airplanes and the history of flight.
ISBN 1-55407-134-8
1. Airplanes -- Juvenile literature. I. Title.
629.133/34 dc22   TL547.O954 2005

Library and Archives Canada Cataloguing in Publication

Oxlade, Chris
   Airplanes : uncovering technology / Chris Oxlade.
Includes index.
ISBN 1-55407-134-8
   1. Airplanes--Juvenile literature. I. Title.
TL547.O94 2006   j629.133'34   C2005-904806-9

AIRPLANES

UNCOVERING TECHNOLOGY

Chris Oxlade

FIREFLY BOOKS

Table of Contents

First Steps to Flight, p. 11

The Need for Speed, p. 34

In the Cockpit, p. 50

Introduction

An airplane streaking across the sky leaving a trail of vapor high above the clouds is an everyday sight for us. Airplanes play an important role in our busy, modern lives. Millions of passengers climb aboard passenger airplanes every day to travel for work and pleasure. Cargo airplanes carry goods and packages all over the world. And military airplanes patrol the skies, lead attacks on enemy positions, deliver supplies to armies on the ground below and help after natural disasters.

An airplane is a flying machine with wings. Just over a hundred years ago there were no airplanes as we know them today. The first fliers rose into the air in lighter-than-air balloons and airships, but these could never be machines for practical mass travel. Once airplanes were flying, they quickly got bigger and faster. During World Wars I and II, and the Cold War, countries needed to build better airplanes than their enemies did. They put huge efforts into developing new airplane technologies, such as radar and jet engines. These technologies were soon seen on civilian airplanes when the conflicts ended. In peacetime there were battles between airplane manufacturers to build the best airliners.

The history of flight is littered with famous airplanes and their famous pilots who made record-breaking flights, flying higher, further and faster than anyone had before. A few pilots, such as Charles Lindbergh, became legends. Other pilots, such as World War I's the Red Baron, are remembered for their deeds during airplane battles. All contributed to the fascinating world of airplanes today.

Myths of flight

Many ancient myths and legends feature heroes who flew like birds. In a famous Greek myth, Daedalus and his son Icarus were captives on the island of Crete. Daedalus made wings from feathers and wax so they could fly to freedom. "Don't fly too high or the sun will melt the wax on your wings," Daedalus warned his son. But Icarus got carried away. He flew higher and higher. The wax melted, his wings fell apart and he plunged into sea and drowned.

Leonardo da Vinci

The Italian scientist and artist Leonardo da Vinci (1452–1519) sketched hundreds of ideas for mechanical devices. Among them were several flying machines, including a parachute, a helicopter with a rotor like a huge screw and an ornithopter. The ornithopter was a machine with wings that were flapped by a person strapped into it. We don't know whether da Vinci ever built any of these machines.

*Leonardo da Vinci drew this flying machine about 500 years ago. The aviator would have laid on his back. The wings (**a**, **b**) would have been flapped up and down by a system of pulleys (**c**, **d**, **e**), operated by the aviator's legs.*

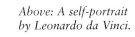
Above: A self-portrait by Leonardo da Vinci.

Learning to Fly

For thousands of years our ancestors must have watched birds swooping effortlessly through the sky and dreamt of copying them. The first people who tried to fly did just that. They strapped birdlike wings to their arms and flapped hard. Sadly, many of these "bird men" plummeted to their deaths. We know now that our bodies are not designed for flight. We must rely on machines to get off the ground.

Joseph (right) and Étienne Montgolfier.

The Montgolfier brothers

The French brothers Joseph and Étienne Montgolfier were famous for their hot-air balloons. Watching smoke rising from a fire, Joseph realized that if rising hot air could be trapped, it might lift a machine into the air. Soon the brothers were building and testing hot-air balloons. On November 21, 1783, François Pilâtre de Rozier, a scientist, and François d'Arlandes, a friend of the Montgolfiers, lifted off in a Montgolfier balloon. They landed 25 minutes later, 5 miles (8 km) from the launch site. They were the first humans to fly.

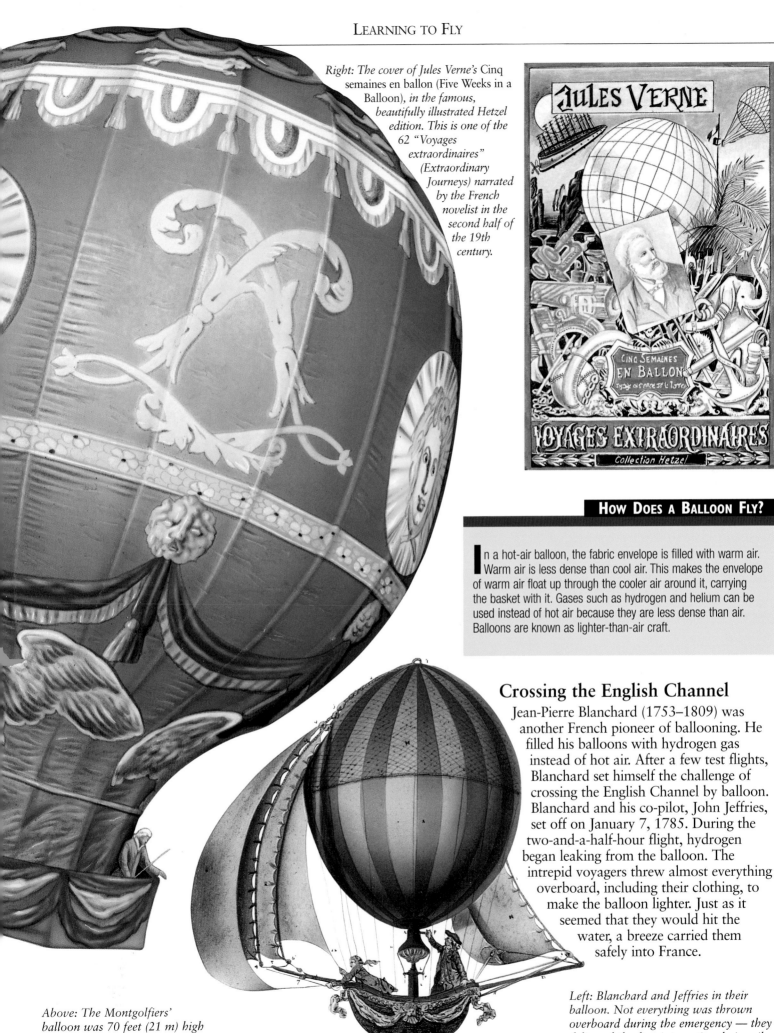

Right: The cover of Jules Verne's Cinq semaines en ballon (Five Weeks in a Balloon), *in the famous, beautifully illustrated Hetzel edition. This is one of the 62 "Voyages extraordinaires" (Extraordinary Journeys) narrated by the French novelist in the second half of the 19th century.*

HOW DOES A BALLOON FLY?

In a hot-air balloon, the fabric envelope is filled with warm air. Warm air is less dense than cool air. This makes the envelope of warm air float up through the cooler air around it, carrying the basket with it. Gases such as hydrogen and helium can be used instead of hot air because they are less dense than air. Balloons are known as lighter-than-air craft.

Crossing the English Channel

Jean-Pierre Blanchard (1753–1809) was another French pioneer of ballooning. He filled his balloons with hydrogen gas instead of hot air. After a few test flights, Blanchard set himself the challenge of crossing the English Channel by balloon. Blanchard and his co-pilot, John Jeffries, set off on January 7, 1785. During the two-and-a-half-hour flight, hydrogen began leaking from the balloon. The intrepid voyagers threw almost everything overboard, including their clothing, to make the balloon lighter. Just as it seemed that they would hit the water, a breeze carried them safely into France.

Above: The Montgolfiers' balloon was 70 feet (21 m) high and 40 feet (12 m) across.

Left: Blanchard and Jeffries in their balloon. Not everything was thrown overboard during the emergency — they delivered the first international airmail.

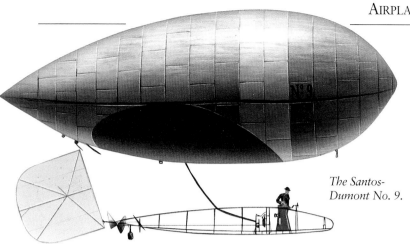

The Santos-Dumont No. 9.

Early dirigibles

The first dirigible was built by Frenchman Henri Giffard in 1852, but its heavy steam engine made it slow and cumbersome. The invention of the lighter and more powerful internal combustion engine made airships more practical. Brazilian Alberto Santos-Dumont (1873–1932) built a series of airships with large gas bags. In 1900 his No. 6 craft won a prize for flying 7 miles (10 km) around the Eiffel Tower in Paris. Von Zeppelin founded his first airship-building company in 1898. From the start he built huge rigid airships with metal frames. His earliest airship, the LZ1, first flew in 1900, but it was difficult to control.

Below: The Hindenburg *over lower Manhattan, New York, in 1936. This was the largest airship ever built.*

Zeppelins

The balloons of the late 1700s and early 1800s allowed people to fly, but they were not a practical form of transportation. They were blown where the wind took them. The answer was the airship, or dirigible. This was a lighter-than-air craft with a propeller to push it along. The age of the airship reached its peak in the 1930s, when vast gas-filled craft carried passengers across the world's oceans and continents. Most successful were the German Zeppelins, the brainchild of Count Ferdinand von Zeppelin.

Crowded skies above Paris are shown on this magazine cover of the early 1900s.

Passengers traveled in style. During the day they sat in the saloon (below) and at night they slept in comfortable couchettes.

Around the world

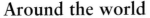

In 1909, von Zeppelin co-founded DELAG, the world's first commercial airline. In 1929 the enormous *Graf Zeppelin* airship began a transatlantic passenger service. It carried 39 passengers nonstop between Germany and New York. To raise publicity for the service, *Graf Zeppelin* (left) completed the first round-the-world flight, taking 29 days for the trip.

The *Hindenburg*

In 1936, a new Zeppelin airship took to the skies. LZ129, named *Hindenburg* after the German chancellor, was 804 feet (245 m) long (more than twice the length of a football field). It could carry 70 passengers on two decks. Its four diesel engines pushed it along at 84 mph (135 km/h) across the Atlantic between Germany, the United States and Brazil. Disaster struck in 1937 when the *Hindenburg* exploded. It was the end of an era.

The Hindenburg *burst into flames on May 6, 1937, as it tried to dock on its mooring tower in Lakehurst, New Jersey. Thirty-five passengers and crew died. Amazingly, 62 survived the inferno.*

Inside an airship

The great airships such as the *Graf Zeppelin* and the Hindenburg had lightweight aluminum frames with huge bags of hydrogen gas inside. The passenger area was built into the bottom of the frame, or hung underneath. Although airships were three times faster than ocean liners, a transatlantic trip still took at least two days.

First Steps to Flight

The knowledge built up by Sir George Cayley (right) and Otto Lilienthal (above) was invaluable to later aviators such as the Wright brothers.

To become a practical form of transport the airplane had to be capable of sustained, controlled flight. The alternative to balloons and airships was the heavier-than-air airplane. It had a lightweight engine to power it through the air and the pilot could steer it, making it climb and dive and turn left and right on command. The first controlled, powered flight was made in 1903 by the Wright brothers' "Flyer." A few powered airplanes had left the ground before this, but they made only short, uncontrolled hops.

Gliders

Two pioneers of glider flight were English scientist Sir George Cayley (1773–1857) and German engineer Otto Lilienthal (1848–1896). Cayley was the first person to understand the basic principles of flight. In 1849 a 10-year-old boy took off in one of Cayley's gliders. He was the first person to fly in a heavier-than-air aircraft. Lilienthal made more than 2,000 flights in his gliders. He hung under the wing, running off a hillside to take off and steering by shifting his body around. He died when one of his gliders crashed.

Samuel Langley, who almost beat the Wrights in their bid to make the first sustained and controlled flight.

The race for the skies

At the end of the 1890s many would-be flyers in the United States and Europe were racing to build a successful airplane. Among them was the American scientist Samuel Langley (1834–1906). He built several model airplanes, including one with a gas engine that was the first airplane to achieve a sustained flight. After this success Langley built a full-scale airplane, called Aerodrome, which he attempted to launch from a houseboat on the Potomac River in October 1903. The launching mechanism failed and the plane plunged into the water. Meanwhile, in North Carolina, bicycle makers Wilbur (1867–1912) and Orville (1871–1948) Wright had spent four years carrying out hundreds of experiments with kites and gliders. They had designed both efficient wings and a way of making a plane climb, dive and turn. They even built their own lightweight gas engine. On December 17, 1903 the Wright's Flyer made the first-ever sustained, controlled flight.

Above and below: The Flyer lifts off for the first time with Orville Wright at the controls. The historic flight lasted just 12 seconds.

European milestones

It was nearly three years after the Wrights made their famous flight that a sustained, powered flight was made in Europe. This was achieved by the Brazilian aviator Alberto Santos-Dumont, the airship pioneer, who had turned his attention to heavier-than-air flight. In October 1906, Santos-Dumont flew 197 feet (60 m) in his airplane, the 14-bis, winning 1,500 French francs from the French aero club in the process. Another famous name in European aviation was Louis Blériot. After several early failures and crashes, Blériot built a monoplane (an airplane with one pair of wings) with an engine at the front and tailplane and fin at the rear. This arrangement is still used on most modern propeller-driven airplanes. In 1909, Blériot crossed the English Channel in his Blériot XI monoplane, winning a prize of £1,000 from the *Daily Mail* newspaper. The 32-minute flight made Blériot a national hero in France.

Left: A poster celebrating French aviator Louis Blériot crossing the English Channel in 1909.

Right: Santos-Dumont's kitelike 14-bis airplane.

Left: The Curtiss biplane (an airplane with two sets of wings) was a typical early airplane. It had a flimsy wooden frame and fabric-covered wings. The front stabilizers controlled climbing and diving, and the rear rudder controlled turning. The pilot sat on the bottom wing, next to the engine.

American milestones

It wasn't until 1908 that Glenn Curtiss (1878–1930) became the next American to build a plane and fly it. In 1910 a Curtiss plane, piloted by Eugene Ely, made the first takeoff from the deck of a ship (right). The next year Ely pulled off the more tricky feat of landing on a ship. Another record for the United States was the world's first airline. It operated in 1914 between St. Petersburg and Tampa, Florida, using a Benoist flying boat (left).

World War I

Military leaders were quick to realize how useful airplanes could be in battle. Airplanes first saw action in 1911 in the war between Italy and Turkey. World War I gave a huge boost to airplane development as new planes that could fly faster and higher were constantly designed. A few World War I pilots became heroes. They were the famous fighter aces.

Above: The Sopwith Camel was Britain's best fighter of World War I. It had a top speed of 115 mph (185 km/h). Sopwith Camels shot down nearly 1,300 enemy planes in 1917–1918.

WHAT WAS WORLD WAR I?

World War I, also called the Great War, was fought in Europe from 1914 to 1918. On one side were France, Britain, Russia, Italy and the United States, known as the Allied Powers. On the other side were Germany, Austria-Hungary and Turkey, known as the Central Powers. The main cause of the war was Germany's aim to become the most powerful nation in Europe. On the Western Front in France and Belgium, conditions in the trenches were horrific. Millions of soldiers were killed by bullets, shells and poisonous gas, gaining and losing a few yards of mud.

Below: Bomb damage in France during World War I.

Right: A British poster telling the public how to identify German planes and to take shelter if they saw one.

The Red Baron

Most famous of all the World War I fighter aces was Baron Manfred von Richthofen (1892–1918). After shooting down an enemy plane with his observer's machine gun, he decided to train as a fighter pilot. Von Richthofen often flew in aircraft painted red, including a Fokker Dr-I, from which he got his nickname "The Red Baron." He was soon given his own squadron of fighters, which became known as von Richthofen's Flying Circus. Von Richthofen survived being shot down twice and was awarded the Blue Max medal before he was killed in action in April 1918. He had shot down 80 enemy planes.

A German pilot releasing a single bomb by hand.

War in the air

The military went into World War I with little or no experience of air warfare. At first aircraft were used simply for reconnaissance (see opposite page). Pilots and observers carried guns and rifles in case they met an enemy plane. Single-seat fighters such as the British Sopwith Camel were developed to shoot down enemy reconnaissance planes. Fighters were designed to climb fast and turn tightly, and were armed with machine guns. Pilots learned fighting techniques such as attacking with the sun behind them so that the enemy was blinded. They also started flying in organized groups rather than alone.

Bombs away

At the beginning of World War I there were no proper bombers. The first bombs were dropped by hand. A pilot simply leaned over the side of his cockpit and let the bomb go. Hitting the target was almost impossible. The first bombing raid of the war was carried out by a single German plane over Paris in 1914. The next year German Zeppelin airships bombed London. These raids were meant to frighten civilians, but they did little damage. Specialized heavy bombers such as the British Handley Page O/100 and the German Gotha GVb appeared later in the war.

Reconnaissance

Reconnaissance flights were the most common and
important missions during World War I. Pilots, and
the observers who flew with them, were sent
to spy on enemy positions and troop
movements. They also reported on the accuracy
of their own side's artillery and helped them to correct
their aim. Reconnaissance planes carried cameras to
take photographs of the ground. They were always
under threat from the faster enemy fighters trying to
stop them. The observer defended the plane with a
machine gun.

More aces

Britain's most successful World War I fighter ace was
Edward Mannock, with a total of 73 victories over
enemy planes. Mannock joined the Royal Flying
Corps after reading about the exploits of another
British ace, Albert Ball. Mannock was a ruthless fighter and a great
leader and teacher of novice pilots. He was shot down and killed
in July 1918. Francesco Baracca was Italy's leading ace, with 34
victories. After his death his mother presented the family coat of
arms (above) to Enzo Ferrari, the motor manufacturer. It still
appears on every Ferrari car.

*Above: The Fokker
Dr I triplane was Germany's
most famous World War I
fighter. It could climb fast and
turn sharply, making it hard to catch
and difficult to escape from.*

*A fight between two aircraft
was known as a dogfight. Pilots
dodged and swerved, trying to
get the enemy plane into their
gun sights.*

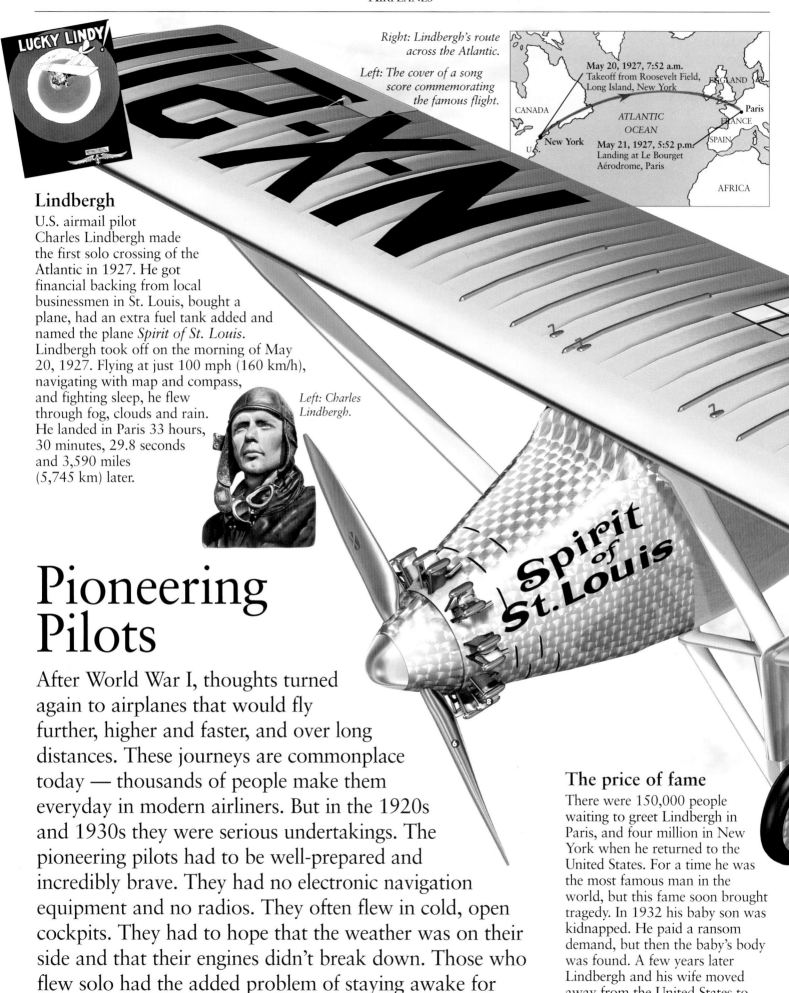

LUCKY LINDY

Right: Lindbergh's route across the Atlantic.

Left: The cover of a song score commemorating the famous flight.

CANADA

May 20, 1927, 7:52 a.m.
Takeoff from Roosevelt Field, Long Island, New York

ENGLAND

Paris

ATLANTIC OCEAN

FRANCE

New York

SPAIN

U.S.

May 21, 1927, 5:52 p.m.
Landing at Le Bourget Aérodrome, Paris

AFRICA

Lindbergh

U.S. airmail pilot Charles Lindbergh made the first solo crossing of the Atlantic in 1927. He got financial backing from local businessmen in St. Louis, bought a plane, had an extra fuel tank added and named the plane *Spirit of St. Louis*. Lindbergh took off on the morning of May 20, 1927. Flying at just 100 mph (160 km/h), navigating with map and compass, and fighting sleep, he flew through fog, clouds and rain. He landed in Paris 33 hours, 30 minutes, 29.8 seconds and 3,590 miles (5,745 km) later.

Left: Charles Lindbergh.

Pioneering Pilots

After World War I, thoughts turned again to airplanes that would fly further, higher and faster, and over long distances. These journeys are commonplace today — thousands of people make them everyday in modern airliners. But in the 1920s and 1930s they were serious undertakings. The pioneering pilots had to be well-prepared and incredibly brave. They had no electronic navigation equipment and no radios. They often flew in cold, open cockpits. They had to hope that the weather was on their side and that their engines didn't break down. Those who flew solo had the added problem of staying awake for endless hours in the air.

The price of fame

There were 150,000 people waiting to greet Lindbergh in Paris, and four million in New York when he returned to the United States. For a time he was the most famous man in the world, but this fame soon brought tragedy. In 1932 his baby son was kidnapped. He paid a ransom demand, but then the baby's body was found. A few years later Lindbergh and his wife moved away from the United States to avoid more publicity.

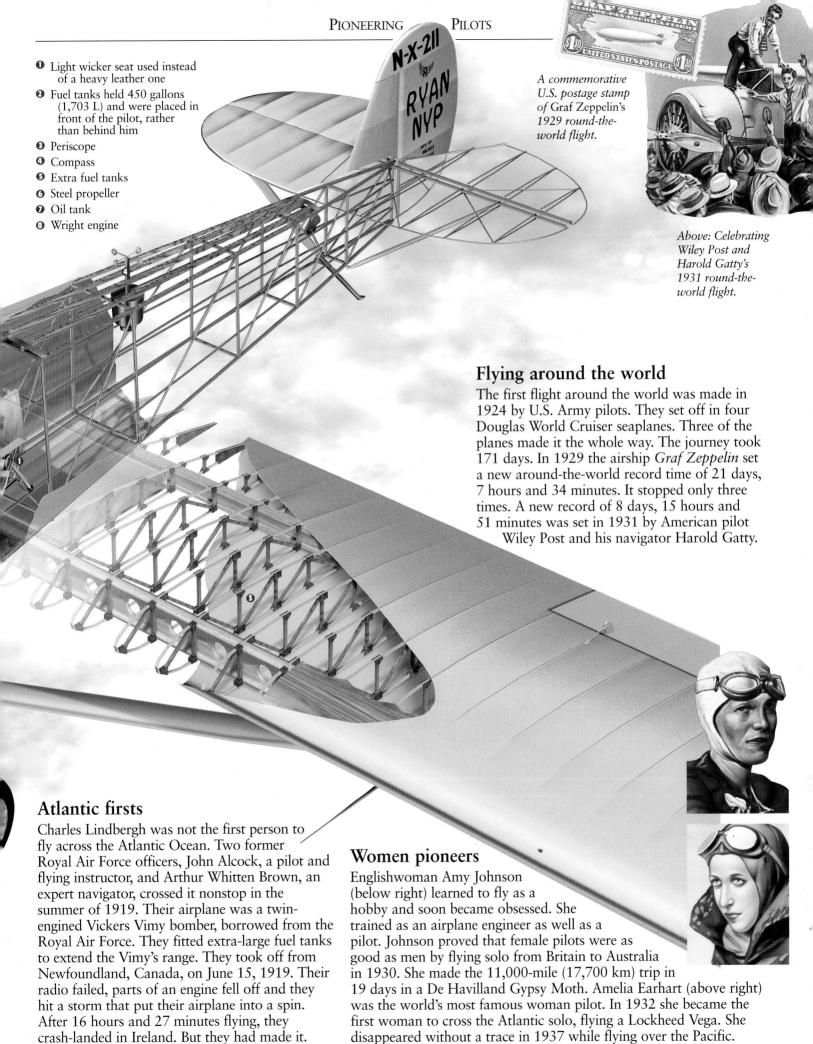

1 Light wicker seat used instead of a heavy leather one
2 Fuel tanks held 450 gallons (1,703 L) and were placed in front of the pilot, rather than behind him
3 Periscope
4 Compass
5 Extra fuel tanks
6 Steel propeller
7 Oil tank
8 Wright engine

A commemorative U.S. postage stamp of Graf Zeppelin's 1929 round-the-world flight.

Above: Celebrating Wiley Post and Harold Gatty's 1931 round-the-world flight.

Flying around the world

The first flight around the world was made in 1924 by U.S. Army pilots. They set off in four Douglas World Cruiser seaplanes. Three of the planes made it the whole way. The journey took 171 days. In 1929 the airship Graf Zeppelin set a new around-the-world record time of 21 days, 7 hours and 34 minutes. It stopped only three times. A new record of 8 days, 15 hours and 51 minutes was set in 1931 by American pilot Wiley Post and his navigator Harold Gatty.

Atlantic firsts

Charles Lindbergh was not the first person to fly across the Atlantic Ocean. Two former Royal Air Force officers, John Alcock, a pilot and flying instructor, and Arthur Whitten Brown, an expert navigator, crossed it nonstop in the summer of 1919. Their airplane was a twin-engined Vickers Vimy bomber, borrowed from the Royal Air Force. They fitted extra-large fuel tanks to extend the Vimy's range. They took off from Newfoundland, Canada, on June 15, 1919. Their radio failed, parts of an engine fell off and they hit a storm that put their airplane into a spin. After 16 hours and 27 minutes flying, they crash-landed in Ireland. But they had made it.

Women pioneers

Englishwoman Amy Johnson (below right) learned to fly as a hobby and soon became obsessed. She trained as an airplane engineer as well as a pilot. Johnson proved that female pilots were as good as men by flying solo from Britain to Australia in 1930. She made the 11,000-mile (17,700 km) trip in 19 days in a De Havilland Gypsy Moth. Amelia Earhart (above right) was the world's most famous woman pilot. In 1932 she became the first woman to cross the Atlantic solo, flying a Lockheed Vega. She disappeared without a trace in 1937 while flying over the Pacific.

Above: U.S. mail was first carried by air in 1911, by pilot Earl Ovington.

Right: A poster advertising the U.S. airmail service.

The birth of airmail

Airmail services began in the United States, where the huge distances between cities made mail deliveries very slow. The U.S. Postal Service asked people to bid for contracts to operate set airmail routes. Regular services began in 1918. Most routes were operated using converted single-engine World War I biplanes. At first some routes were run by U.S. Army airplanes. People who posted mail could pay a premium for their letter or package to go by airmail. On average, mail traveled three times faster by air than by train.

Flying at night

To make airmail services efficient, pilots had to fly at night. But this was impossible because they could not see enough to navigate. In the United States this was solved by building lines of beacons for pilots to follow. The system worked in all but the worst weather. In low visibility they often kept going anyway, following railway lines lit up by their landing lights. Even so, it was easy for a pilot to become disoriented and many went into spinning dives and crashed. This difficulty was overcome by the introduction of instruments that showed when the plane was turning and banking.

Left: Beacons like this sent out beams of radio waves that planes could detect.

By 1939, the Douglas DC-3 was carrying three-quarters of all the passengers from the United States. It was converted into a military transport plane in World War II.

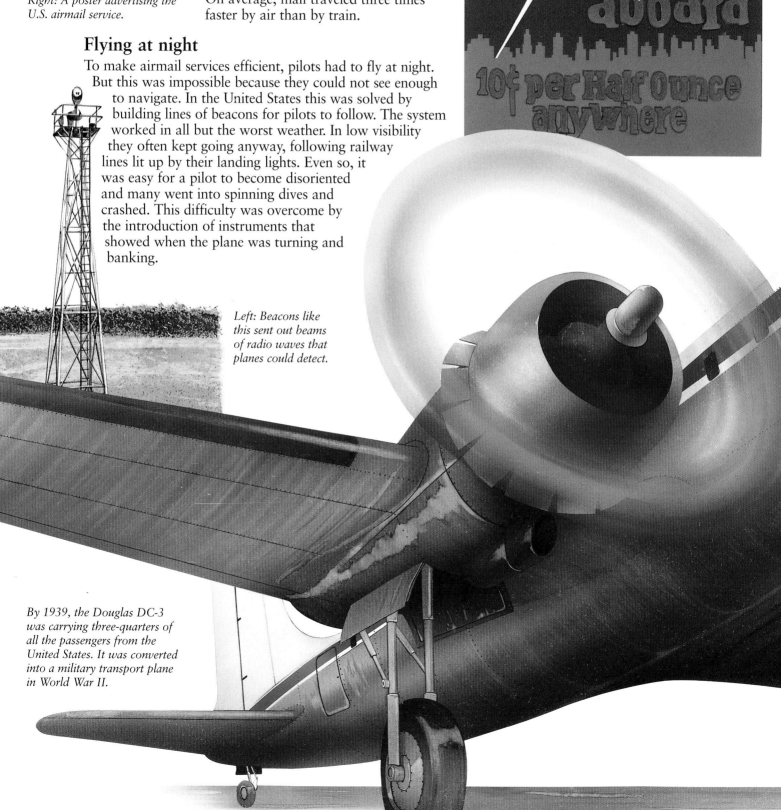

There goes the AirMail is your Letter aboard 10¢ per Half Ounce anywhere

The Birth of Airlines

Commercial aviation took off soon after World War I. There were plenty of ex-military airplanes and pilots to start up airmail and passenger services. The need to fly regularly on long-distance routes drove the development of new technologies. Airplanes became larger and faster, and engines became more reliable. Radio navigation equipment and other new instruments allowed pilots to fly safely at night and in poor weather.

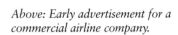

Above: Early advertisement for a commercial airline company.

Above left: The all-metal Ford Tri-motor of 1926 could carry 13 passengers. It was known as the Tin Goose.

Below: The Boeing B-80 carried 18 passengers.

From post to passengers

In the early 1920s, when airmail services were proving to be a success, there were hardly any passenger services. The airplanes of the time could carry only one or two passengers, making fares expensive. Far more money could be made by carrying the same weight in mail. The first crude airliners were converted World War I bombers. Traveling in them was cold, noisy and bumpy. Conditions improved when the first proper airliners, such as the Ford Tri-motor and Boeing B-80, were introduced.

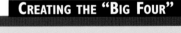

The bigger the better

There was competition for passengers among the big airlines. Each one wanted new airliners that would carry more passengers, faster and in more comfort than their rivals. Experts think of the Boeing 247, introduced in 1933, as the first modern-style airliner. It could carry 10 passengers at 155 mph (250 km/h). In 1936, Douglas introduced the DC-3 to compete. It could carry 21 passengers, and would become one of the most successful airliners of all time. Bigger airliners meant lower fares, and in the 1930s the number of people flying rocketed. By the late 1930s, regular passenger services crisscrossed the world.

CREATING THE "BIG FOUR"

The first airlines were small companies. Some had only one airplane and flew on just one route. Many were unreliable because of breakdowns, and others quickly went bust. In the United States the government solved the problem by forcing small airlines to merge with each other. By 1930 there were four big domestic airlines — American Airlines, Eastern Airlines, United Airlines and TWA — known as the "Big Four." These airlines operated the main long-distance routes across the United States between "hub" airports at major cities. There were still many smaller airlines, but they operated local routes from the main hubs to surrounding towns and cities. At the same time Pan American Airways had started carrying mail and passengers to South America and across the Pacific Ocean using flying boats.

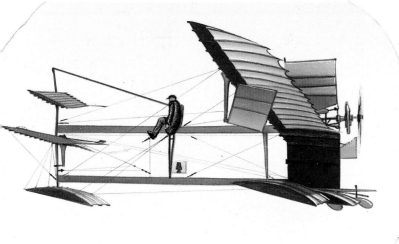

The First Seaplanes

The term "seaplane" is normally used to describe a small airplane with floats instead of a wheeled undercarriage. Larger airplanes with a fuselage shaped like the hull of a boat are usually known as "flying boats." Seaplanes were developed where sheltered bays or large lakes offered huge areas of flat water for takeoffs and landings. In the 1930s, monster flying boats operated on long-distance passenger routes because there were hardly any long, concrete runways for large "land" planes to use.

Early seaplanes

The very first airplane to take off from water was *Hydravion* (above) built by Frenchman Henri Fabre in 1910. In the United States, Glenn Curtiss built a series of seaplanes, the first of which flew in 1911. In 1912 Curtiss sold 150 seaplanes to the U.S. Navy, which used them to observe enemy ship movements. An annual race for seaplanes, the Schneider Trophy, started in 1912. This led to the development of fast seaplanes, some of which held the world airspeed record.

Above and right: Ads for Pan America's Boeing Clipper Service.

A Boeing 314 Clipper taking off.

Right: Inside the luxurious passenger cabin and dining room of the Dornier Do X flying boat. There were cabins with bunks and bathrooms, too.

The Catalina

The most successful of all the flying boats was the Consolidated PBY Catalina. It first flew in 1935. Catalinas were designed for the U.S. Navy as flying patrol boats. They played a vital part in World War II, flying reconnaissance missions, rescuing pilots who had crashed into the sea and bombing and torpedoing enemy ships and submarines. The Catalina was robust and reliable and had machine guns to defend itself. More than 4,500 Catalinas were built. Later models of the Catalina were amphibious, which means they could also land on runways using a retractable undercarriage.

Rise and fall of the flying boat

By the end of the 1930s flying boats offered the best of luxury intercontinental travel. The Boeing 314 Clipper was the largest passenger flying boat ever built. It carried up to 74 passengers in spacious cabins. Pan American operated mail and passenger services with the Clipper from the United States to Europe and the Asia. Britain's largest flying boat was the Shorts C-class Empire, operated by Imperial Airways on routes to Australia. By the end of World War II, long-range bombers and transport aircraft had been developed, and there were plenty of long runways. The era of the flying boat was over.

Above: An advert for the England-to-Australia service of Qantas Empire Airways.

World War II Fighters

Air power was to have a huge impact during World War II. In the 1930s, Germany had built up a large fleet of fighters and bombers. This air force was called the Luftwaffe and it was the strongest in the world. Other countries built up their air forces in preparation for war. While armies, navies and air forces fought overseas, designers and engineers at home tried to build new airplanes that would give their pilots the edge over the enemy.

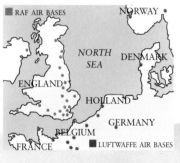

Above: World War II British and German air bases.

The Battle of Britain

In 1940 the Germans planned to invade Britain. The Luftwaffe launched attacks on British airfields, air force command centers and radar stations. British Royal Air Force (RAF) fighters, mainly Hawker Hurricanes and Supermarine Spitfires, tried to shoot the bombers down. By the end of the summer of 1940, the RAF was losing more planes than could be built to replace them. Then German bombers accidentally hit homes in London. The British retaliated with raids on Berlin. The Germans switched their attack to London on purpose, allowing the RAF to recover. The Germans called off the invasion in 1941 because they were losing so many planes over Britain. The Battle of Britain was won. "Never was so much owed by so many to so few," said Winston Churchill of the RAF's fighter pilots.

Britain's wartime leader Winston Churchill.

ABOUT WORLD WAR II

World War II (1939–1945) began when Germany, Italy and Japan tried to become more powerful by invading their neighbors. Together these countries were known as the Axis. Other countries, mainly Britain, the United States and Russia, known as the Allies, tried to stop them.

In Europe the war started when Germany, led by Adolf Hitler's Nazi Party, invaded Poland. With a force led by fighters and bombers, the invasion lasted only four weeks. France fell just as quickly. The war spread to Africa, Russia, the Far East and the Pacific. From 1942, the German and Japanese forces were gradually pushed back. They finally surrendered in 1945.

A ground crew prepares a Hawker Hurricane fighter for its next mission.

The Mitsubishi A6M Zero.

Right: A Japanese Zero burning during the attack on Pearl Harbor.

Pearl Harbor

On December 7, 1941, the Japanese attacked Pearl Harbor, the U.S. Naval base on the Pacific island of Hawaii. Japan attacked because it expected that the United States' powerful navy would prevent its expansion in the Pacific. In all, 423 fighters and fighter-bombers, such as the Mitsubishi Zero, took part in the attack, which was launched from six aircraft carriers. Japanese bombs and torpedoes sank and damaged 18 ships, and destroyed 300 aircraft. Only 29 Japanese fighters were lost. The Zero was the best Japanese fighter of the war. More than 10,000 were built. Its only weak point was its poor armor. Pearl Harbor demonstrated the power of carrier-based aircraft.

The American P-51 Mustang, probably the best fighter on any side in the war.

The birth of radar

Radar stands for "radio detecting and ranging." Radar equipment sends out a beam of radio waves called microwaves. Any waves that hit an object, such as an airplane, bounce back, allowing radar equipment to work out the position and distance of the object. A working radar system had just been developed when World War II began. In Britain, radar gave the RAF warning of bombers approaching from France, allowing fighters time to take off and intercept them.

Defending the night skies

With the Battle of Britain over and the United States in the war after Pearl Harbor, Allied air strength began to grow. The Allies built up a huge fleet of long-range bombers and began to attack cities in Germany. The bombers had no fighter support, and were picked off by German fighters such as the Messerschmitt Bf 109 and the Focke-Wulf 190. Night fighters were fitted with onboard radar to spot bomber formations in the dark. Eventually, long-range escort fighters such as the P-51 Mustang flew with the bombers. The Mustang was the world's fastest propeller-driven fighter when the war ended.

Left: A modern radar system.

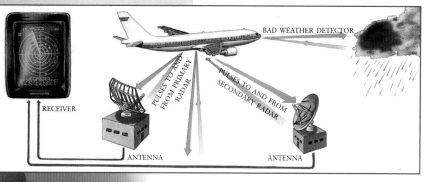

BAD WEATHER DETECTOR

RECEIVER

PULSES TO AND FROM PRIMARY RADAR

PULSES TO AND FROM SECONDARY RADAR

ANTENNA

ANTENNA

Inventing the jet engine

Two men developed jet engines almost at the same time. Neither knew about the work of the other. In Germany, scientist Hans von Ohain (left) began work on a jet engine in 1935, when he was only 24. He had an engine working in 1937. Working with airplane builder Ernst Heinkel, he built an experimental plane, the Heinkel He 178, which made the first flight by a turbojet-powered airplane in 1939. Meanwhile, in Britain, Frank Whittle (right), a British RAF officer and engineer, had the idea for a jet engine in 1929, but only started experimenting in 1937. By 1941 a prototype jet airplane was flying with one of Whittle's engines.

The Jet Engine

During the 1940s a new sound was heard in the skies. The deep hum of the piston engine was gradually replaced by the screeching roar of the jet engine. During World War II, piston-engined fighters had become faster and faster, but the higher the speed, the less efficient propellers became. About 450 mph (725 km/h) was the top speed they could manage. The jet engine (properly called the turbojet) was the answer to the problem. It works by pushing a stream of hot gases backward. This pushes the engine and the airplane forward. Unlike the piston engine, the jet engine is most efficient at high speeds.

The Messerschmitt Me 262.

Early jet planes

The first mass-produced jet airplane was the twin-engine Messerschmitt Me 262 fighter. The prototype flew in 1941. But the engines often caught fire and their turbine blades broke. German engineers also had difficulty in getting the materials they needed for the engine parts. These problems meant that the Me 262 didn't start fighting until 1944. It was much faster than any other fighter of the time and had some success shooting down Allied bombers. But it could only fly for an hour before running out of fuel, and its engines had to be replaced regularly.

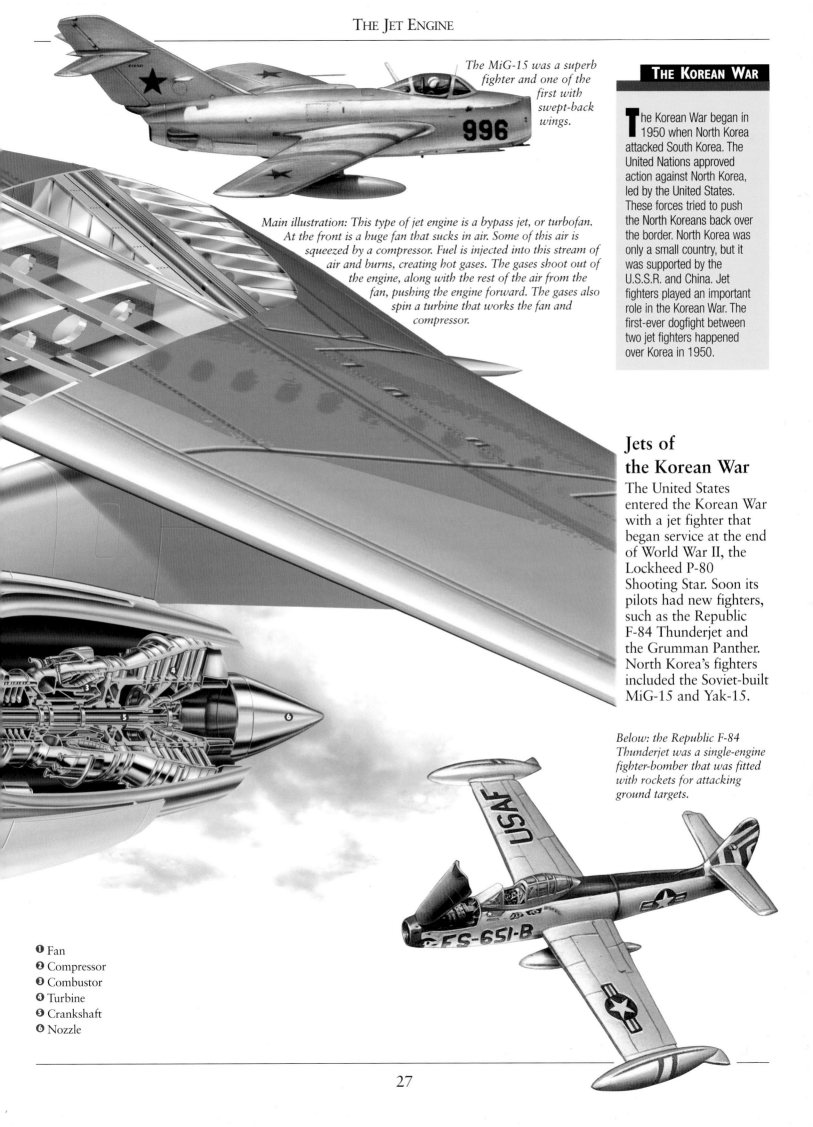

The MiG-15 was a superb fighter and one of the first with swept-back wings.

Main illustration: This type of jet engine is a bypass jet, or turbofan. At the front is a huge fan that sucks in air. Some of this air is squeezed by a compressor. Fuel is injected into this stream of air and burns, creating hot gases. The gases shoot out of the engine, along with the rest of the air from the fan, pushing the engine forward. The gases also spin a turbine that works the fan and compressor.

THE KOREAN WAR

The Korean War began in 1950 when North Korea attacked South Korea. The United Nations approved action against North Korea, led by the United States. These forces tried to push the North Koreans back over the border. North Korea was only a small country, but it was supported by the U.S.S.R. and China. Jet fighters played an important role in the Korean War. The first-ever dogfight between two jet fighters happened over Korea in 1950.

Jets of the Korean War

The United States entered the Korean War with a jet fighter that began service at the end of World War II, the Lockheed P-80 Shooting Star. Soon its pilots had new fighters, such as the Republic F-84 Thunderjet and the Grumman Panther. North Korea's fighters included the Soviet-built MiG-15 and Yak-15.

Below: the Republic F-84 Thunderjet was a single-engine fighter-bomber that was fitted with rockets for attacking ground targets.

❶ Fan
❷ Compressor
❸ Combustor
❹ Turbine
❺ Crankshaft
❻ Nozzle

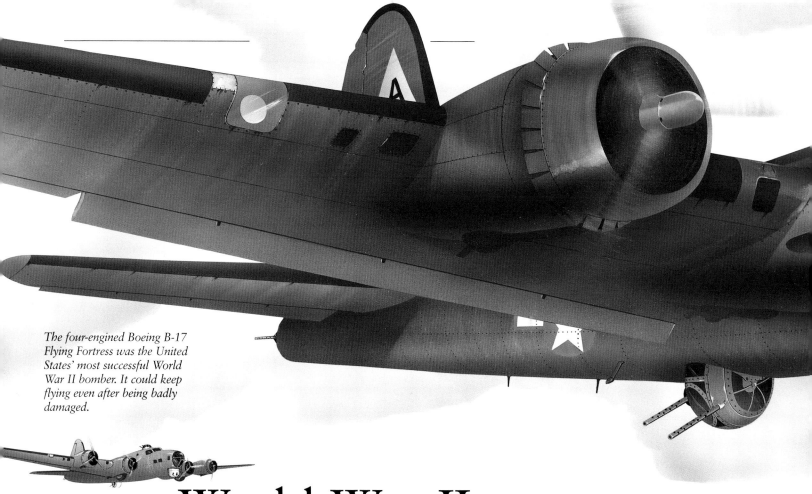

The four-engined Boeing B-17 Flying Fortress was the United States' most successful World War II bomber. It could keep flying even after being badly damaged.

World War II Bombers

Below: Posters designed to keep up people's morale during the Blitz.

Bombers played an important role in World War II. They destroyed enemy positions and armor, enemy ships and airplanes, enemy industries, infrastructure such as railway depots and ports, and enemy cities. There was a wide range of bombers. The heavy bombers carried tons of bombs to drop on enemy targets. They dropped their bombs from thousands of feet up and were not always very accurate. Light bombers and fighter-bombers often carried just one bomb or torpedo which they fired at close range. Bomber crews could only expect to fly a few missions before being shot down.

BRITAIN SHALL NOT BURN

THE ATTACK BEGINS IN THE FACTORY

The Blitz

Between September 1940 and May 1941 German bombers attacked London night after night. This period is known as the Blitz. For 57 consecutive days, from September 7 to November 3, 1940, London was bombed every single night or day. The German bombers were the Dornier Do-17, Heinkel He-111 and Junkers Ju-88. They hit at industrial targets such as factories and docks, and also at the rest of the city to try to frighten and demoralize London's population. The city suffered massive damage. Many buildings were destroyed, but some, such St. Paul's Cathedral (below), survived. Thousands of people were killed in their homes, but many more were saved by hiding in air-raid shelters.

UNDERGROUND

BETHNAL GREEN

THIS WAY TO THE AIR RAID SHELTER

Above: London's subway stations were used as air-raid shelters. People slept on the station platforms.

Bombs around the clock

Starting in 1942, British and American bombers began an almost continuous bombing campaign against German industrial areas such as the Ruhr valley. The raids were designed to disrupt weapon making and so reduce the effectiveness of the German forces. Together the Allies decided that American bombers would fly missions during the day and British bombers would fly at night. This round-the-clock bombing would allow the German air defenses and fighter pilots no rest. The U.S. Air Force wanted to fly by day so they could drop their bombs more accurately. They defended themselves by flying in box formation, but they suffered heavy losses.

Below: The B-29 Flying Fortress had machine guns mounted in rotating turrets.

Left: The Avro Lancaster, the Dambusters' bomber.

Allied assault on Germany

The Allies eventually decided to launch massive bombing raids on German cities to try to demoralize the German people. The missions were flown by bombers such as British Wellingtons and American B-29 Superfortresses. They flew in huge formations, often of more than a thousand bombers. Air commanders believed these huge raids would overwhelm the German defenses. Some German cities were reduced to rubble. In one raid on Hamburg in 1943, the bombs caused firestorms so hot that the streets melted. Forty thousand people died.

The Dambusters

Bomber pilots often staged special missions against particular targets. The pilots of the most famous of these raids are known as the Dambusters. Their mission was to destroy dams in the Ruhr. A special bouncing bomb was developed for the job because normal bombs would not damage the immense concrete dams. The Lancaster bombers flew low, each releasing a bomb that bounced across the water like a skimming stone, hit the dam, sank down and exploded. Two dams were breached, knocking out power supplies to industries for several months.

Dropping the atomic bomb

During World War II several countries raced to develop an atomic bomb. The United States had the first bomb ready in 1945. The Allies decided to drop it on Japan to try to make Japan surrender. They knew that thousands of people would die, but they thought millions would die on both sides if they tried to invade Japan. The first atomic bomb was dropped on Hiroshima on August 6, 1945, from a B-29 Superfortress called *Enola Gay*. Hiroshima was almost completely destroyed. Eighty thousand people died instantly. Japan surrendered after another bomb was dropped on Nagasaki three days later.

Commercial Airliners Take Off

By the end of World War II, airplane manufacturers were building tens of thousands of military airplanes every year. When the war ended fewer airplanes were needed. The manufacturers of bombers and transport airplanes, such as Boeing, Douglas and Lockheed, began to think about building passenger airliners. They started with piston-engine airliners, such as the Boeing Stratocruiser, Douglas DC-7 and Lockheed Constellation. Early jet engines were very inefficient, but they gradually improved. When jet airliners were introduced in the 1950s they quickly became popular with airline chiefs and passengers. The piston-engine airplanes quickly disappeared, and by the early 1960s jet airliners ruled the skies.

Below: A de Havilland Comet in the colors of the British airline BOAC.

A troubled start

The first jet airliner to carry passengers was the Comet, built in Britain by de Havilland. It made its maiden flight in 1949 and entered service with the airline BOAC in 1952. Everything went well until 1954, when a Comet broke up in flight at 30,000 feet. Soon after, the same accident happened to another Comet. All Comets were grounded (banned from flying). The airplane was redesigned and began flying again four years later.

Main illustration: A DC-3. The first versions of this transport airplane, called Douglas Sleeper Transports, began service in 1936.

LONG HAUL COMFORT

Being a passenger in a jet airliner was far more comfortable than being a passenger in a piston-engined airliner. Most weather happens in the lowest layer of the atmosphere. Flying here can be bumpy as the air swirls around. Jet engines can work at a much higher altitude than piston engines, which allows airliners to fly above the weather. Also gone was the noise and vibration from the piston engines. As well, jet airliners were twice as fast as piston-engine airliners, making flight times shorter. Soon jet airliners were flying nonstop across the United States and the Atlantic Ocean.

A certificate given to passengers on the maiden passenger flight of the BOAC Comet.

Boeing vs. Douglas

In the 1950s there was a tough battle between the American airplane manufacturers Boeing and Douglas Aircraft to produce the first successful jet airliners. Boeing's success had come from building military bombers and jet fighters. Douglas was the world's leading airliner manufacturer, with planes such as the DC-7. Seeing the success of the Comet, both companies decided to build a jet airliner. It was a risk, but success would mean getting orders from the big American airlines. The airlines — especially the largest one, Pan American — knew that competition between Boeing and Douglas would mean they would get a good aircraft. They needed airliners that would carry many passengers efficiently. Boeing created the 707 and Douglas the DC-8.

Left: A cutaway of a Boeing 707 airliner. It was the first airplane to have engines mounted on struts under the wings. It also had wings that were swept back at an angle. Most modern airliners have the same design.

The first jet airliners

In 1952 Boeing designed an airplane that could be both a military tanker and an airliner. The first version of the 707, called the Dash-80, flew in 1954. The U.S. Air Force bought dozens of the tanker version of the airplane. Boeing then built the airliner version. Douglas started designing the DC-8 airliner in 1955. It first flew in 1958. Both airplanes could fly nonstop across the Atlantic.

Below: The four-engined Douglas DC-8 looked very similar to the Boeing 707. It could carry 175 passengers.

Short and medium haul

Designed as long-distance airliners, when the Boeing 707 and the Douglas DC-8 entered service with the airlines they flew long routes between major cities. On medium and short routes the airlines used piston and turboprop airliners. In the late 1950s Boeing developed the three-engined 727. A new, faster jet airplane for medium-range routes, it could take off from short runways at smaller airports and climb and descend quickly to get the maximum time cruising at high altitude. Douglas didn't build a competitor to the 727, but in 1963 it decided to build a short-range airliner, the DC-9. Boeing's short-range airliner was the 737. Modern versions of these airliners are still being built.

Cold War Planes

During World War II the alliance between the Soviet Union (U.S.S.R.) and the other Allies was not very strong. When the fighting finished, Germany and other parts of Europe were divided into two halves. East Germany was controlled by the Soviet Union and West Germany by the United States, Britain and France. Then the communist U.S.S.R. also took control of its neighbors, including Poland and Czechoslovakia, forming what was known as the Soviet Bloc. There was deep mistrust between the two sides, and they almost stopped communicating. The Cold War had begun. Each side developed airplanes for spying on the other side and for carrying their nuclear bombs in case war broke out.

Not-so-secret spy plane

The most famous spy plane of the Cold War was the American Lockheed U-2. It flew over the U.S.S.R. 65,000 feet (20,000 m) up, well out of range of guns on the ground, photographing troop movements, airfields and missile-launching stations. In May 1960 a U-2 was shot down over the U.S.S.R. by a missile. The United States refused to apologize for spying. In return the U.S.S.R. called off peace talks in Paris. The U-2 pilot, Gary Powers, survived and was held captive until he was exchanged for a Soviet spy in 1962.

The Lockheed U-2.

ABOUT THE COLD WAR

The Cold War is a term used to describe the disagreements and tensions between the Western powers and the Soviet Bloc that existed through the 1950s and into the 1960s. The Cold War was not a real war, but it might easily have turned into one. If it had, it could have been catastrophic because each side had a huge stock of nuclear weapons permanently aimed at the other. Both sides were prepared for war, and their airplanes were vital. Long-range bombers carried nuclear bombs ready to be dropped. Each side spied on the other with reconnaissance planes.

The Berlin airlift

World War II left Berlin divided into a Soviet sector, an American sector, a British sector and a French sector. The city was surrounded by land controlled by the U.S.S.R. In 1948 the United States, Britain and France decided to join their sectors into one and introduce a new currency. The U.S.S.R. didn't like the idea and set up a blockade to prevent food, fuel and other supplies getting into the Allied sectors. In reply, the Allies organized what is now known as the Berlin airlift. Using USAF and RAF transport planes, they flew an average of more than 600 flights per day, delivering two million tons of supplies. The Soviets lifted the blockade in 1949.

Round-the-clock threat

During the Cold War each side had enough nuclear weapons to destroy the other many times over. They used their nuclear weapons as a deterrent, knowing that the other side was unlikely to attack because there would be instant retaliation. In case of attack, there would be very little warning, so both sides kept bombers with nuclear weapons in the air 24 hours a day, 365 days a year. The jet-powered bombers were refueled in flight by tanker planes so they could stay in the air longer. The Unites States operated the immense eight-engined Boeing B-52 Stratofortress, and the U.S.S.R. operated bombers such as the Tupolev Tu-16.

Above: Two Tupolev Tu-16 bombers.

Above: Nikita Khrushchev was prime minister of the U.S.S.R. from 1958 to 1964, in the later part of the Cold War. He tried to maintain peace by visiting the United States.

Above: A B-52 refueling from a KC-135 Stratotanker (the tanker version of the Boeing 707 airliner).

Below: The Lockheed SR-71 Blackbird, a spy plane with a top speed of 2,000 mph (3,200 km/h), which could fly at 85,000 feet (26,000 m).

The Cuban Missile Crisis

In 1959 Fidel Castro became leader of the Caribbean country of Cuba. Castro was a communist. The U.S. government was unhappy about having a communist state so close to it own shores. In 1961, it helped anti-Castro rebels to land at the Bay of Pigs in Cuba and try to take over the country. The attempted invasion failed badly. Castro then invited the U.S.S.R. to build nuclear missile launching sites in Cuba. In 1962, the building sites were spotted by U.S. spy planes, and American President John F. Kennedy demanded the missiles be taken back to the U.S.S.R. After a few days of tension the U.S.S.R agreed. This incident is known as the Cuban Missile Crisis.

A Cuban exile in the United States watching news of the 1962 Cuban Missile Crisis on television.

The Need for Speed

As the speeds of their fighters increased, pilots started to encounter problems. Their planes began to vibrate badly and their controls stopped working. Some pilots were killed when they got into high-speed dives and couldn't pull out. Sometimes the buffeting was so bad that planes broke up in the air. These problems happened because the planes were approaching the speed of sound. When aeronautical engineers solved these problems, the age of supersonic fighters, bombers and airliners began.

Above: Breaking the sound barrier.

Below: A famous feature of the Concorde is the drooping nose. This was raised in flight, and lowered during takeoff and landing so that the pilot could see the runway.

The Concorde has a delta-shaped wing, which gives good performance both at supersonic speeds and low speeds. It is powered by four jet engines with afterburners to push it through the sound barrier. Top speed is Mach 2.2 (about 1,360 mph or 2,200 km/h).

Breaking the sound barrier

American aeronautical engineers began to investigate the problems of control at high speed. They decided to build a research airplane that would have the power to reach and then break through the sound barrier. The result was the Bell X-1. It was built in the shape of bullet because engineers knew that a bullet could fly faster than sound, and it was powered by a rocket engine. It was carried into the air by a converted Boeing B-29 rather than taking off normally.

The Concorde

With supersonic fighters flying, manufacturers of commercial airliners began to think about building supersonic transport planes (SSTs). The only SST to carry passengers was the Concorde. It was a joint project between the British Aircraft Corporation and the French company Sud-Aviation. Design work began in 1963, with the maiden flight in 1969. The Concorde entered service with Air France and BOAC in 1976. About 14 Concordes flew, mainly between London, Paris and New York. Because of a crash in 2000 and falling passenger numbers, the Concorde was retired in 2003.

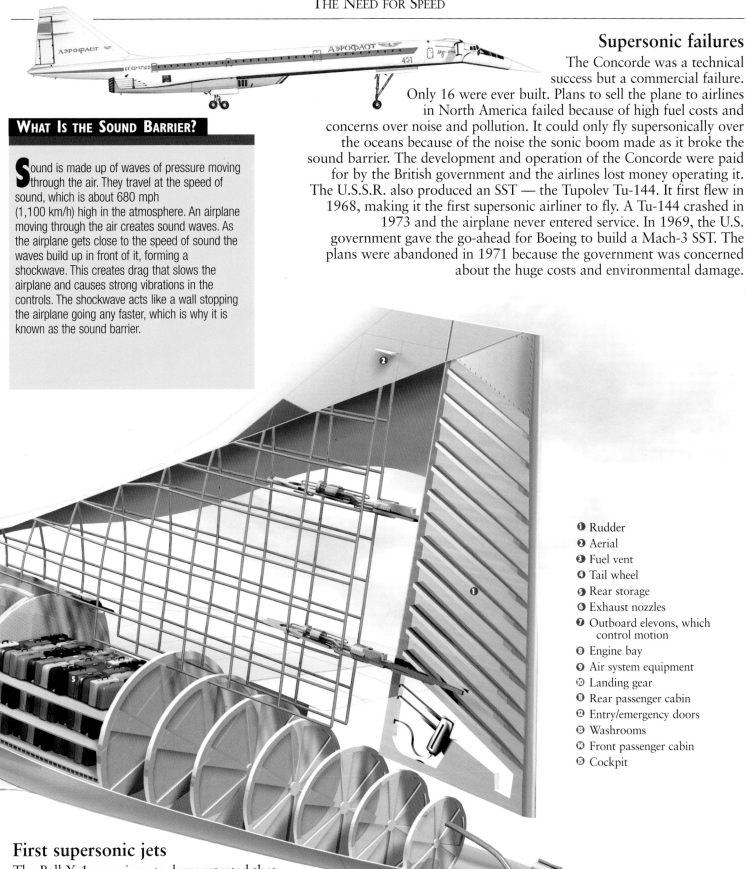

Supersonic failures

The Concorde was a technical success but a commercial failure. Only 16 were ever built. Plans to sell the plane to airlines in North America failed because of high fuel costs and concerns over noise and pollution. It could only fly supersonically over the oceans because of the noise the sonic boom made as it broke the sound barrier. The development and operation of the Concorde were paid for by the British government and the airlines lost money operating it. The U.S.S.R. also produced an SST — the Tupolev Tu-144. It first flew in 1968, making it the first supersonic airliner to fly. A Tu-144 crashed in 1973 and the airplane never entered service. In 1969, the U.S. government gave the go-ahead for Boeing to build a Mach-3 SST. The plans were abandoned in 1971 because the government was concerned about the huge costs and environmental damage.

WHAT IS THE SOUND BARRIER?

Sound is made up of waves of pressure moving through the air. They travel at the speed of sound, which is about 680 mph (1,100 km/h) high in the atmosphere. An airplane moving through the air creates sound waves. As the airplane gets close to the speed of sound the waves build up in front of it, forming a shockwave. This creates drag that slows the airplane and causes strong vibrations in the controls. The shockwave acts like a wall stopping the airplane going any faster, which is why it is known as the sound barrier.

❶ Rudder
❷ Aerial
❸ Fuel vent
❹ Tail wheel
❺ Rear storage
❻ Exhaust nozzles
❼ Outboard elevons, which control motion
❽ Engine bay
❾ Air system equipment
❿ Landing gear
⓫ Rear passenger cabin
⓬ Entry/emergency doors
⓭ Washrooms
⓮ Front passenger cabin
⓯ Cockpit

First supersonic jets

The Bell X-1 experiments demonstrated that supersonic airplanes were a possibility. Research into high-speed flight continued, with rocket-powered experimental X-planes in the United States reaching Mach 2 (twice the speed of sound). In the meantime, manufacturers were developing supersonic jet fighters. The first jet fighter to break the sound barrier was the North American F-86 Sabre, but it had to go into a dive to do it. The F-86 was the first American fighter with swept-back wings. Engineers had realized that angling the wings back toward the tail moved them out of the way of the shockwave from the airplane's nose. This reduced the vibration of the wings near the sound barrier. The F-100 Super Sabre was the first aircraft capable of level supersonic flight. It had afterburners in its engines, which provided extra thrust to push it through the sound barrier.

Boeing 747: the Jumbo Jet

Boeing announced that it was going to build the 747 in 1966. The new plane would be so big that Boeing's existing factory was too small. The company had to build a new factory, which was the world's largest building. When the first plane rolled out, Boeing already had more than 150 orders from Pan Am, Japan Air Lines and Lufthansa in Germany. Because of its size, the 747 was quickly nicknamed the Jumbo Jet. The first version of the 747 carried nearly 400 passengers. Several new versions have appeared since. The 747-300 has a stretched upper deck. The latest model, the 747-400, has winglets on its wing tips to improve efficiency. It can carry up to 568 passengers. So far Boeing has built more than 1,200 Jumbos.

A Pan Am poster advertising its new Boeing 747s.

A Qantas 747 coming in for a landing.

The 747's upper deck made it stand out from other airliners. Overall the plane is 229 feet (70 m) long and as high as a six-story building.

Bigger Is Better

The commercial airline industry was changed for good on February 9, 1969, when the Boeing 747, or Jumbo, airliner made its first flight. The new 747 was similar to the Boeing 707, with four engines mounted on the wings. The difference was in the fuselage. It was wide enough for 10 passengers to sit across — far wider than any previous airliner. A new term was made up for this new sort of airplane — the wide-body airliner. The 747 and the other wide-body airliners created a huge rise in the number of passengers flying because they could carry passengers more efficiently, making fares lower.

The DC-10

When McDonnell Douglas first planned the DC-10 it was going to be a four-engined plane carrying 650 passengers. In the end it was a three-engined plane that could carry 380 passengers. All three engines are at the rear and one is under the tail. The DC-10 first went into service in 1970 with American Airlines. It was the main competitor to the Boeing 747. In all, 446 DC-10s were made. The more modern McDonnell Douglas MD-11 was developed from the DC-10.

Keeping up with Boeing

After Boeing's success with its first jet airliner, the 707, it became the leading airliner manufacturer. It followed up with the 727 and the 737. The other U.S. airliner makers, Douglas and Lockheed, struggled to keep up. Douglas had its DC-8 and DC-9, but in the late 1960s was in financial trouble. It was rescued by joining with McDonnell, another airplane maker, to become McDonnell Douglas. Both McDonnell Douglas and Lockheed decided to build their own wide-body jets, but they were two years behind Boeing. McDonnell Douglas created the DC-10 and Lockheed the L-1011 Tristar. Both flew for the first time in 1970. Both had three engines, were slightly smaller than the 747 and carried fewer passengers. Unfortunately they competed against each other rather than the 747.

Many airliners are also produced in cargo form. Federal Express operates a fleet of DC-10 cargo planes to carry parcels.

Right: A Lockheed Tristar taking off from Hong Kong. The Tristar was the only jet airliner that Lockheed ever made.

Right: Airbus A300

Below: Airbus A340

European wide-body jets

In Europe there was no airplane manufacturer large enough to challenge Boeing or McDonnell Douglas. But in 1965 manufacturers from Britain, France, Spain and Germany joined forces and formed Airbus Industries. Its first airliner was a medium-range wide-body airliner called the Airbus A300 that could carry 250 passengers. It first flew in 1972. It was also the first twin-engine wide-body airliner. Airbus also made the A310, which is shorter than the A300 but can fly further. In 1987 Airbus set out to make two new wide-body airliners, the A330 and A340. Both airplanes have the same fuselage and wings. The A330 has two engines. The A340 has four smaller engines, giving it greater range. In the U.S.S.R. the Ilyushin company developed its own wide-body airliner, the Il-86.

Vietnam War in the air

Both sides used airplanes in the Vietnam War. The Americans dropped millions of tons of bombs. Napalm bombs were used to burn villages where the Americans thought enemy fighters were hiding. They attacked enemy troops with fighter-bombers such as the McDonnell F-4 Phantom and Douglas A-4 Skyhawks, which operated from aircraft carriers and airfields. North Vietnamese pilots fought them in Soviet fighters such as MiG-17s and MiG-19s.

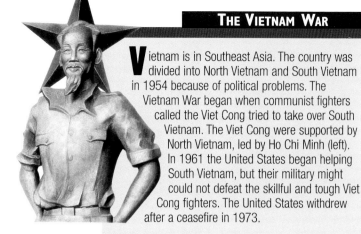

THE VIETNAM WAR

Vietnam is in Southeast Asia. The country was divided into North Vietnam and South Vietnam in 1954 because of political problems. The Vietnam War began when communist fighters called the Viet Cong tried to take over South Vietnam. The Viet Cong were supported by North Vietnam, led by Ho Chi Minh (left). In 1961 the United States began helping South Vietnam, but their military might could not defeat the skillful and tough Viet Cong fighters. The United States withdrew after a ceasefire in 1973.

Left: A C-130 Hercules dropping a tank out from its cargo ramp while flying low and slow.

The Hercules

The hilly, jungly landscape of Vietnam made it difficult for the United States to supply its troops by road. The Lockheed C-130 Hercules cargo plane came to the rescue. It was designed to take off from and land on short, rough, temporary runways. The Hercules has a high wing and high tailplane, which create space for a rear cargo ramp and a huge cargo bay. There is enough room inside for two tanks.

Vertical take off

A vertical take off and landing (VTOL) airplane can take off and land vertically, like a helicopter, but also fly like a normal airplane. In the 1950s, military airplane designers realized that a VTOL jet fighter could operate almost anywhere, from a small forest clearing to an aircraft carrier. The first VTOL plane to fly was the British Hawker Siddeley P.1127, which first took off in 1961. It was developed into the Harrier, which entered service with the RAF in 1969. The Harrier was nicknamed the "jump jet" because of its vertical takeoffs.

Vietnam and Beyond

Airplanes were used in new ways during the Vietnam War. They were armed with new weapons, such as air-to-air missiles and air-to-surface missiles. They were given sophisticated electronics for aiming weapons and for navigating. Pilots developed new tactics for fighting in their supersonic fighters. World War II had shown that aircraft carriers were vital for fighting a war overseas. In Vietnam, hundreds of American fighters and bombers operated from carriers. Airplanes were also important in other conflicts, such as the Six-Day War in Israel (1967) and the Falklands War (1982).

Left: A Harrier taking off. The engine exhaust comes out through swiveling nozzles. The nozzles are turned to point down for takeoff and landing, and turned to point backward for normal flight.

Above: An Israeli McDonnell F-4 Phantom. This U.S.-built plane had two crew members, a pilot and a navigator, who also fired the air-to-air missiles stored under its wings. The Phantom's top speed was Mach 2.2.

War in Israel

Air power had a huge effect on two wars in the Middle East. The Six-Day War was fought in 1967. Israel had built up a powerful air force, mainly of French airplanes, like the Dassualt Mirage. The Arab countries around it were armed with Soviet airplanes, including the MiG-19 and MiG-21. On June 5, 1967, Israeli planes made a surprise attack on Egyptian air bases, destroying many of Egypt's planes. They attacked airfields in Jordan, Iraq and Syria, too. The strikes prevented attacks from the air on Israel's army, which was invading part of Syria. The Yom Kippur War started in 1973 with air attacks on Israel from Egypt, Syria and Iraq. Israel responded but many of its planes were shot down by surface-to-air missiles (SAMs). Israeli pilots attacked the SAM launchers with another new weapon, the guided air-to-surface missile.

The Falklands War

In April 1982 Argentinian troops invaded the British Falkland Islands, off the coast of Argentina. Britain sent a task force to take the islands back. Britain could not use airfields in South America. Instead, it sent long-range Vulcan bombers (left) on bombing missions from Ascension Island, nearly 4,000 miles (6,500 km) away in the mid-Atlantic. Vertical-takeoff Harriers operated from two aircraft carriers, bombing and attacking Argentinian ground troops on the islands. The Harriers were also good in air-to-air combat because the pilots could turn sharply using the thrusters. Argentina's most successful weapon was the Exocet anti-ship missile, which could be fired from an airplane up to 20 miles (32 km) from its target. Exocets sank two British warships. By destroying the only runway on the islands, the British prevented Argentinian planes from defending their troops. The Harriers could still operate and the British forces re-took the islands.

Below: The Boeing E-3 AWACS. Its radar is in the saucer mounted on its back. Inside is a team of air controllers.

The Boeing 777

The last large airliner to enter service in the 20th century was the Boeing 777. It is a wide-body, twin-engine airliner that can carry 300–350 passengers on long haul routes. The 777's turbofan engines are the most powerful jet engines ever made. Each one is as powerful as five of the engines that powered Boeing's first jet airliner, the 707. These huge engines are contained in pods that are as wide as a 737 fuselage. Modern engines are very reliable. Twin-engine airplanes are now allowed to cross oceans because the chances of both engines failing at once are so small.

Main illustration: F/A-18

Planes of Today

Modern airplanes, especially military jets and passenger airliners, are extremely high-tech machines. Electronics and computers do many of the jobs that pilots once did. Computer monitors, or "glass cockpits," have replaced many of the old dials and gauges, and electronic voices warn pilots of problems. Electronic systems help fighter pilots to target their weapons and defend themselves. Some weapons are aimed simply by looking at the target. Recent conflicts in the Persian Gulf, Yugoslavia and Afghanistan have featured air strikes by these high-tech machines and their accurate weapons. Advanced fighters and airliners are actually flown by computers with systems known as "fly-by-wire." The fighters would be impossible to fly without them because they are so unstable in flight. They are designed this way for high maneuverability.

Electronic warfare

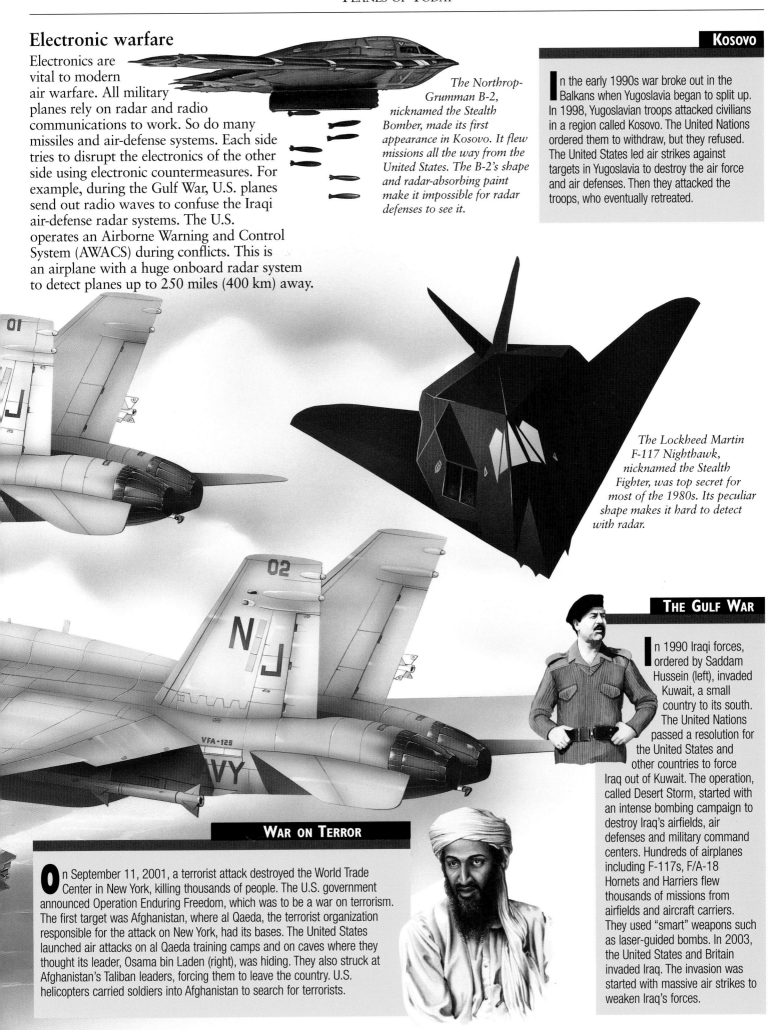

Electronics are vital to modern air warfare. All military planes rely on radar and radio communications to work. So do many missiles and air-defense systems. Each side tries to disrupt the electronics of the other side using electronic countermeasures. For example, during the Gulf War, U.S. planes send out radio waves to confuse the Iraqi air-defense radar systems. The U.S. operates an Airborne Warning and Control System (AWACS) during conflicts. This is an airplane with a huge onboard radar system to detect planes up to 250 miles (400 km) away.

The Northrop-Grumman B-2, nicknamed the Stealth Bomber, made its first appearance in Kosovo. It flew missions all the way from the United States. The B-2's shape and radar-absorbing paint make it impossible for radar defenses to see it.

Kosovo

In the early 1990s war broke out in the Balkans when Yugoslavia began to split up. In 1998, Yugoslavian troops attacked civilians in a region called Kosovo. The United Nations ordered them to withdraw, but they refused. The United States led air strikes against targets in Yugoslavia to destroy the air force and air defenses. Then they attacked the troops, who eventually retreated.

The Lockheed Martin F-117 Nighthawk, nicknamed the Stealth Fighter, was top secret for most of the 1980s. Its peculiar shape makes it hard to detect with radar.

THE GULF WAR

In 1990 Iraqi forces, ordered by Saddam Hussein (left), invaded Kuwait, a small country to its south. The United Nations passed a resolution for the United States and other countries to force Iraq out of Kuwait. The operation, called Desert Storm, started with an intense bombing campaign to destroy Iraq's airfields, air defenses and military command centers. Hundreds of airplanes including F-117s, F/A-18 Hornets and Harriers flew thousands of missions from airfields and aircraft carriers. They used "smart" weapons such as laser-guided bombs. In 2003, the United States and Britain invaded Iraq. The invasion was started with massive air strikes to weaken Iraq's forces.

WAR ON TERROR

On September 11, 2001, a terrorist attack destroyed the World Trade Center in New York, killing thousands of people. The U.S. government announced Operation Enduring Freedom, which was to be a war on terrorism. The first target was Afghanistan, where al Qaeda, the terrorist organization responsible for the attack on New York, had its bases. The United States launched air attacks on al Qaeda training camps and on caves where they thought its leader, Osama bin Laden (right), was hiding. They also struck at Afghanistan's Taliban leaders, forcing them to leave the country. U.S. helicopters carried soldiers into Afghanistan to search for terrorists.

Boeing Sonic Cruiser

In 2001, Boeing announced plans for a completely new type of airliner, the Boeing Sonic Cruiser. Most large jet airliners cruise at about Mach 0.8. The Sonic Cruiser was intended to fly at Mach 0.98. Without having to break through the sound barrier, the Sonic Cruiser would reduce flight times on long-haul routes by about 20 percent. Boeing scrapped the Sonic Cruiser program in 2002 because of the huge costs of developing the needed technology. It has decided to concentrate on building more efficient conventional airliners.

Left: The Boeing Sonic Cruiser

Below: The RQ-4A Global Hawk Unmanned Reconnaissance System.

❶ Turbofan engine
❷ Aperture radar

Future fighters

A new generation of fighters is entering into service. In the United States, the F-22 Raptor will fly with the U.S. Air Force from 2005. It features hidden weapons bays to make it stealthy, and swiveling engine nozzles for high maneuverability. A new vertical takeoff and landing fighter, the F-35 is being developed. Before long, fighters will be flying with no pilots. The Unmanned Combat Air Vehicles (UCAVs) will fly and use their weapons automatically. The Northrop-Grumman X-47 Pegasus is a pilotless stealth fighter being tested in the United States. Pilotless spy planes have already been used in recent conflicts in Afghanistan and Iraq. They are called Unmanned Reconnaissance Air Vehicles (URAVs).

Below: The X-47 Pegasus will operate from aircraft carriers, taking off and landing automatically. It will be used for reconnaissance and air attacks on the ground.

The Next Generation

The newest airplanes of today will be flying for at least another 20 years. At the moment there are only two manufacturers building large airliners — Boeing in the United States and Airbus Industries in Europe. It looks as though they will continue making conventional airliners for many years to come. They will work hard to make new models more efficient, quieter and easier for pilots to fly in the increasingly crowded skies. It is likely that the Boeing 777 will still be in production in 2050, and still flying in 2100. Boeing has also updated the 737, a plane designed in the 1960s. At the moment there are no plans for a supersonic airliner.

Replacing the shuttle

The space shuttle first flew into space in 1981. NASA is researching new ways of getting astronauts into space and back, especially to the International Space Station. In 1996, Lockheed began to develop the X-33 or Venture Star, a test vehicle for a new generation of space launch vehicle. The design was for a single-stage vehicle. This means that it would not have external fuel tanks or rocket boosters like the shuttle. It would take off vertically using rocket engines and land like a plane. The project was scrapped in 2001 because of technical problems and the huge cost. More than $900 million had already been spent.

❸ Transmitter
❹ Receiver unit
❺ Antennae bay

Above: The North American X-15 was built for research into flying at hypersonic speeds. It was rocket powered and is still the fastest plane of all time, with a record 4,534 mph (7,300 km/h), or Mach 6.72, in 1967.

AIR FORCE

Going hypersonic

In theory there is no limit to the speed at which an aircraft can fly. Since the 1950s, aeronautical researchers have dreamed of building a plane that could fly at Mach 10 or more, and even fly into space. There are big problems flying at hypersonic speeds (speeds greater than about Mach 5). The outside of a plane becomes incredibly hot because of friction with the air, and normal jet engines cannot work. Researchers are trying to build a new type of engine called a supersonic combustion ramjet (scramjet). NASA's current experimental space-plane project is the X-43 or Hyper-X.

Double decker airliner

In 2000, Airbus Industries announced that they were planning to build the world's first true double-deck airliner, the Airbus A380. It is the biggest airliner ever built, with a wingspan of 262 feet (80 m) and a maximum takeoff weight of 617 tons (560 metric tons). The A380's two huge decks run the full length of the plane and have almost twice as much space as a Boeing 747, with room for one-third more seats. The standard A380 carries 555 passengers and the short-range version 656 passengers. Despite its size, the A380 is quieter and more efficient than current airliners. Boeing is planning new versions of the 747 that will compete with the A380.

Above: some A380s have a spacious lower deck with a lounge, bar and area for business-people to work.

A model of the A380.

QANTAS

Early ideas

Leonardo da Vinci was probably the first person to think of the helicopter. He sketched a machine (right) with a spiral air screw about 500 years ago. Frenchman Louis Breguet built a four-rotor helicopter that lifted off the ground in 1907. Another Frenchman, Pierre Cornu, built a two-rotor helicopter that flew soon after. Neither flight lasted more than a few seconds, and the machines only rose a few feet into the air. Other experimental helicopters followed, but they were dangerous, fragile and uncontrollable machines.

Right: The autogyro was invented by Spaniard Juan de la Cierva in 1923. As an autogyro flies along, its unpowered rotor spins automatically, supporting it.

Main illustration: The Hughes 500-D, a successful North American LOH (Light Observation Helicopter).

Helicopters

The first experimental helicopters were built about 100 years ago. But there were many technical problems to sort out and the first practical helicopters did not arrive until 40 years later. A helicopter stays in the air using thin blades like wings joined together to make a rotor. As the rotor spins, the blades cut through the air, creating lift. They work even when the helicopter isn't moving, so a helicopter can take off and land vertically and can also hover.

HK·1354·W

The first helicopter that could be flown under control was the Focke-Wulf Fw 61, designed by Germany's Heinrich Focke. This machine first flew in 1936. It had side-by-side rotors to lift it into the air and a propeller to move it forward.

The first military helicopters

The Focke-Wulf Fw 61 flew well but was too heavy to carry passengers or cargo. Focke developed the Focke-Achgelis Fa 266, a new helicopter based on the Fw 61. This twin-rotor, six-seater transport helicopter first flew in 1940 and was used occasionally in World War II. Developed by Igor Sikorsky, a Russian engineer working in the United States, the Sikorsky XR-4 (left) was the first helicopter designed for military service.

Sikorsky had built the first successful single-rotor helicopter in 1940. It featured a small, vertical rotor at the end of a long tail. This made a sideways push that stopped the fuselage spinning the opposite way of the rotor.

The Sikorsky XR-4 first flew in 1942. It was used near the end of World War II as a transport helicopter. The U.S. Navy experimented with using them on ships.

Transport, search and rescue

Helicopters are perfect for transporting people and cargo to places where conventional planes cannot land. For example, helicopters carry workers to oil rigs at sea and to city-center heliports. Larger transport helicopters, such as the CH-47 Chinook, have two main rotors and no tail rotor. Helicopters are also perfect for search and rescue at sea and in the mountains, where they can hover to pick casualties up from the sea or hillside. The first dedicated rescue helicopter was the Sikorsky S-61, which became known as the Sea King. Helicopters also act as "air" ambulances.

The modern helicopter

By the end of World War II the helicopter had proved what a useful machine it was. Many companies began to design them. One of them was the American company Bell. The first helicopter it manufactured was the Bell Model 47, a two-seater single-rotor machine. The rotor had two blades that made a "chop-chop" sound as it spun, which is why people gave the helicopter the nickname "chopper." The Bell 47 is thought of as the first modern-style helicopter.

The Bell Model 47. It was easily recognized by the glass bubble over the small cockpit.

Helicopters at war

Armies, navies and air forces all use helicopters. Their main job is to transport troops and equipment quickly around the battlefield. Combat helicopters work as attack aircraft. They are armed with machine guns, cannon, rockets and missiles. The first war where helicopters played an important role was the Korean War (1950–1953). In Vietnam helicopters transported troops, acted as flying gunships and rescued pilots from enemy territory. Naval helicopters fly from ships, searching for ships and submarines and attacking them with torpedoes.

Future helicopters

The Comanche is the shape of things to come in the military helicopter world. This machine first flew in 1996 and will enter service in 2006. The Comanche is a "stealth" combat helicopter built with advanced materials and electronics. It is armed with hidden missiles and a machine gun aimed by the pilot's eye.

In the Cockpit

Pilots fly the airplane from the cockpit or flight deck using many controls and instruments. In this cockpit from a 1960s aircraft, clock-type instruments measure air speed, altitude, direction and fuel levels. In newer planes, small computer screens show the same information.

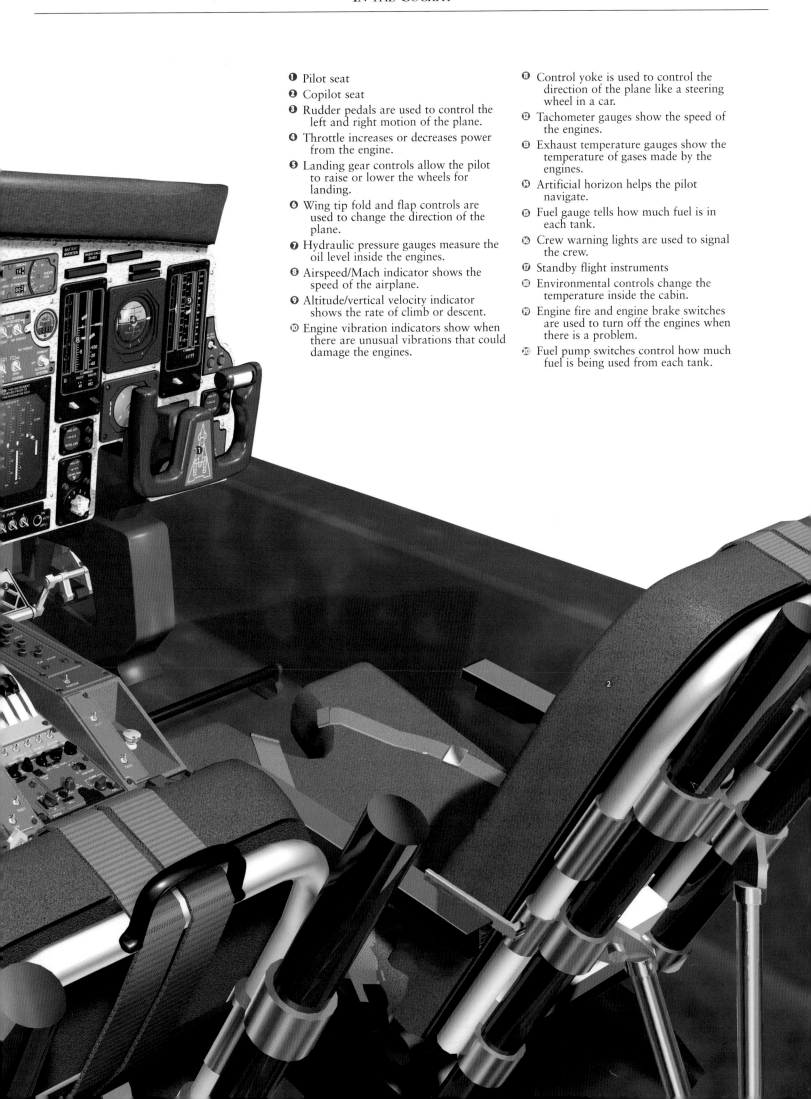

❶ Pilot seat

❷ Copilot seat

❸ Rudder pedals are used to control the left and right motion of the plane.

❹ Throttle increases or decreases power from the engine.

❺ Landing gear controls allow the pilot to raise or lower the wheels for landing.

❻ Wing tip fold and flap controls are used to change the direction of the plane.

❼ Hydraulic pressure gauges measure the oil level inside the engines.

❽ Airspeed/Mach indicator shows the speed of the airplane.

❾ Altitude/vertical velocity indicator shows the rate of climb or descent.

❿ Engine vibration indicators show when there are unusual vibrations that could damage the engines.

⓫ Control yoke is used to control the direction of the plane like a steering wheel in a car.

⓬ Tachometer gauges show the speed of the engines.

⓭ Exhaust temperature gauges show the temperature of gases made by the engines.

⓮ Artificial horizon helps the pilot navigate.

⓯ Fuel gauge tells how much fuel is in each tank.

⓰ Crew warning lights are used to signal the crew.

⓱ Standby flight instruments

⓲ Environmental controls change the temperature inside the cabin.

⓳ Engine fire and engine brake switches are used to turn off the engines when there is a problem.

⓴ Fuel pump switches control how much fuel is being used from each tank.

Index